Editor's Comment

The Future of Energy- Oil and Gas to Remain Dominant- Renewable Energies and Nuclear Expected To Increase Their Share

According to HE Mohammad Sanusi Barkindo, OPEC Secretary General, the future of energy is a future laden with challenges and uncertainties, but also opportunities, however, one thing stakeholders agree on is the fact that the world will need more energy in the decades to come. It is easy to appreciate why.

All of the three main primary sources of energy – oil, gas and coal – will still supply more than three-quarters of the energy mix by 2040. Oil will be at just over 25 per cent, with coal slightly less, and gas slightly more.

From the perspective of oil and gas, it underscores the fact that they will remain central to supplying the growing global population with the critical energy it needs in the decades ahead.

The OPEC Secretary General do not see any outlook predicting that renewables will come close to overtaking oil and gas in the decades ahead. However, these renewable energies and nuclear are expected to increase their share in the energy mix from 18 per cent in 2015 to 22 per cent by 2040.

Mexico Largest Importer of U.S. Natural Gas by Pipeline. Argentina Largest Consumer of U. S.LNG Export by Vessel. Mexico No 1 Destination for U. S. Natural Gas Export by Truck. Canada Top Destination for U. S. Natural Gas Export by CNG- get more analysis in this edition.

Ineos Olefins and Polymers Europe receives U. S. first shipment of ethane. U.S. crude Oil now exports to 16 countries and Canada, however challenges remains- find out more in this news pack edition.

The international pipeline, oil and gas safety conference March 14-16, 2017, seeks to address process safety issues in the upstream, midstream and downstream subsectors of the industry; with special focus on process safety, pipeline safety, and new regulatory impact. Early registration ends Dec. 28, 2016. Conference agenda out! – get a copy @ http://oilandgassafetyconference.com

- Gloria Towolawi

Contents

USA Oil and Gas Monitor
A RGT Media Communications Corp.

Editor-in-Chief
Gloria Towolawi

Europe Bureau
Esther Coker

Nigeria Bureau
David Arhavbarien

Contributing Editor
Gloria Instead

Reporter
Caleb Motinwo

Advert & Marketing
Jewel Spring
T: 832-486-0095
E: advertise@usaoilandgasmonitor.com

Distribution & sales
Richard Godfirst

Subscribers Service
E: subscribe@usaoilandgasmonitor.com

RGT Media Communications Corp.
Publishers of
USA Oil and Gas Monitor
Workplace Weekly News
GlobalPRPlus

USA Oil and Gas Monitor is published 12 times a year monthly by RGT Media Communications Corp. 10777 Westheimer #1100

Houston, Texas 77042
Subscription price is $144 per year. Digital copy $9.99 per download.

Copyright 2016 by
RGT Media Communications Corp.

International Energy Agency

Secure • Sustainable • Together

IEA Urges Japan to Decarbonize its Energy Supply

Japan should balance and diversify its energy mix through a combination of renewable and nuclear energy and efficient thermal power generation, the International Energy Agency IEA said in its latest review of Japan's energy policies, stressing this would help the country build a more secure, affordable, safe and decarbonized energy system.

Japan's energy policy has been dominated in recent years by its efforts to overcome the impact from the 2011 Great East Japan earthquake and the subsequent Fukushima nuclear accident. The accident resulted in the gradual shutdown of all of Japan's nuclear power plants. This in turn led to a significant rise in fossil fuels use, increased fuel imports and rising carbon dioxide emissions. It also brought electricity prices to unsustainable levels.

Speaking at the launch of the IEA's report in Tokyo, IEA Deputy Executive Director Paul Simons acknowledged that since the Fukushima accident, Japan's energy system has shown great resilience. "The traditional focus on security of supply has worked," Mr Simons said. "The future challenge, however, is more about climate change. Japan should take concrete steps to meet its 2030 climate target and to cut emissions significantly more by 2050."

The IEA report encourages Japan to increase low-carbon sources of power supply. Renewable energy supply should become more cost-effective over time. It should also have a broader technological and geographical focus. Nuclear power should gradually be restored but only once the highest safety standards are met and public trust is regained.

The report also highlights Japan's long tradition of effective policies and measures related to energy efficiency. These include the voluntary action plans in industry and the Top Runner Program for appliances, equipment and vehicles. Japan is also adopting gradually stricter building codes and introducing Net Zero Energy requirements for buildings. Both renewables and energy efficiency contribute to increasing energy security.

The IEA applauds Japan for its commitment to energy innovation. The country is not only a major importer and consumer of energy, but also a recognized leader in energy technology development. "Globally, new technologies will be needed to significantly reduce CO_2 emissions beyond 2030," Mr Simons said. "With its strong science and technology base, Japan can make a virtue out of this necessity."

The IEA also urges Japan to fully implement its intended electricity and gas market reforms. It will be essential to ensure that the regulator and competition authority are adequately resourced. Additional infrastructure is needed in the electricity sector for creating a well-integrated national grid, and the market should be designed to give strong signals to locate generation where it is most valuable to the whole system. In the long term, a fully independent transmission system operator should be established.

OPEC Monthly Oil Report shows Brent/WTI Spread Widened Further to $2.36/b

Oil Major Market Highlights from the report reveals the following:

Crude Oil Price Movements — Brent/WTI spread widened, OPEC Basket Rose to $43.10

The OPEC Reference Basket rose 42¢ to $43.10/b in August. ICE Brent ended up 62¢ at $47.16/b, while NYMEX WTI was unchanged at $44.80/b. The Brent/WTI spread widened further to $2.36/b in August. Crude price rose on signs of an improving supply/demand balance and US dollar weakness, although a surprise build in US crude stocks, increasing supplies and worries about Chinese demand pressured prices at the end of the month.

World Economy - GDP growth forecast at 2.9 per cent for 2016 and 3.1 per cent for 2017

World economic growth was revised down to 2.9 per cent for 2016 and remains at 3.1 per cent for 2017. Weak 1H16 growth caused a downward revision to the US growth forecast for 2016 to 1.5 per cent, while the 2017 forecast remains at 2.1 per cent. Growth in Japan was also revised down to 0.7 per cent given weak 1H16 growth. Euro-zone growth remains unchanged at 1.5 per cent for this year and 1.2 per cent for 2017. Forecasts for China and India are also unchanged at 6.5 per cent and 7.5 per cent for 2016 and 6.1 per cent and 7.2 per cent for 2017. The figures for Brazil and Russia remain unchanged from the August MOMR, with growth forecast at 0.4 per cent and 0.7 per cent respectively for next year.

World Oil Demand pegged at 1.23 mb/d

World oil demand growth in 2016 is now anticipated to increase by 1.23 mb/d after a marginal upward revision, mainly to reflect better-than-expected OECD data for the first half of the year. Oil demand in 2016 is expected to average 94.27 mb/d. In 2017, world oil demand is anticipated to rise by 1.15 mb/d, unchanged from the August MOMR, to average 95.42 mb/d. The main growth centers for next year continue to be India, China and the US.

October 2016 • Issue 10

World Oil Supply - Expectations for OPEC NGLs Production Remain Unchanged

Non-OPEC oil supply in 2016 is now expected to contract by 0.61 mb/d, following an upward revision of 0.18 mb/d from the August MOMR to average 56.32 mb/d. This has been mainly due to a lower-than-expected decline in US tight oil and a better-than expected performance in Norway, as well as the early start-up of Kashagan field in Kazakhstan. In 2017, non-OPEC supply was revised up by 0.35 mb/d to show growth of 0.20 mb/d to average of 56.52 mb/d, mainly due to new production from Kashagan. OPEC NGLs are expected to average 6.43 mb/d in 2017, an increase of 0.15 mb/d over the current year. OPEC output, according to secondary sources, dropped by 23 tb/d in August to 33.24 mb/d.

Product Markets and Refining Operations - Strong US gasoline demand reaching around 9.7 mb/d, the highest level seen in years

Product markets in the Atlantic Basin strengthened in August. Refining margins were supported by the positive performance at the top of the barrel due to strong gasoline demand and export opportunities to the EU, as well as concerns about weather disruptions from tropical storms and flooding in the US Gulf Coast. In Asia, margins showed a slight recovery on the back of firm demand and falling inventories ahead of autumn maintenance.

Tanker Market - Dirty tanker spot freight rates the lowest levels seen so far this year

Dirty tanker spot freight rates remained under pressure in August, with negative developments among all classes. VLCC, Suexmax and Aframax spot freight rates declined by 12 per cent, 30 per cent and 14 per cent since July. The drop in rates was mainly driven by excess tonnage supply due to new deliveries at a time when cargo loading requirements remain limited. Stock Movements OECD total commercial stocks fell in July to stand at 3,091 mb, some 341 mb above the latest five-year average. Crude and product inventories showed surpluses of 200 mb and 141 mb, respectively. In terms of days of forward cover, OECD commercial stocks in July stood at 66.1 days, around 7 days higher than the seasonal average.

Balance of Supply and Demand

Demand for OPEC crude in 2016 is estimated to stand at 31.7 mb/d, some 1.7 mb/d over last year. In 2017, demand for OPEC crude is forecast at 32.5 mb/d, an increase of 0.8 mb/d over the current year.

BLM Takes Important Step toward Online Oil and Gas Lease Sales

The Bureau of Land Management BLM has announced that it is implementing authority provided by Congress giving the agency the flexibility to conduct online lease sales. The move is a continuation of the BLM's ongoing efforts to modernize the oil and gas program by increasing program efficiency and generating savings for taxpayers.

The BLM is acting in response to authority provided by Congress as part of the National Defense Authorization Act NDAA for Fiscal Year 2015, which amended the Mineral Leasing Act to allow the BLM to conduct online lease sales. Prior to that amendment, the Mineral Leasing Act authorized Federal onshore oil and gas lease sales only by oral auctions. As result, the BLM's existing regulations referred only to oral auctions. Today's rule modifies those regulations to make clear that, as provided by the NDAA, either internet-based or oral auction procedures are permissible.

This final procedural rule and the legislative changes that preceded it are based on the results of a successful online auction pilot conducted by the BLM in Colorado in 2009. Based on the results of that pilot, the BLM estimates that internet-based auctions could increase aggregate lease sale revenues by about $2 million a year. The BLM believes that online sales have the potential to generate greater competition by making participation easier, which has the potential to increase bonus bids.

The BLM's Eastern States Office will hold the first auction under this new authority on Sept. 20, 2016, when it offers 14 parcels encompassing 4,398 acres of Federal mineral estate in Kentucky and Mississippi. The BLM is evaluating other opportunities to hold additional online sales.

Because this rule relates solely to agency procedures i.e., which auction process can be used and simply restates the relevant statutory authority, it takes effect immediately upon publication in the Federal Register and is not subject to notice and comment requirements. The rule does not change the eligibility requirements to participate in a lease sale or the competitive auction style employed by the BLM. Leases will still be awarded to the highest bidder based on a sequential and ascending bid auction system.

The BLM manages more than 245 million acres of public land, the most of any Federal agency. This land, known as the National System of Public Lands, is primarily located in 12 Western states, including Alaska. The BLM also administers 700 million acres of sub-surface mineral estate throughout the nation. The BLM's mission is to sustain the health, diversity, and productivity of America's public lands for the use and enjoyment of present and future generations. In Fiscal Year 2015, the BLM generated $4.1 billion in receipts from activities occurring on public lands.

October 2016 • Issue 10

Oil and Gas Lease Sales, Fiscal Year 2015

Competitive oil and gas lease sales by BLM State Offices from October 1, 2014 through September 30, 2015.

BLM State Office	Date	Total Receipts*	Parcels Posted[1]	Acres Posted[1]	Parcels Offered Day of Sale[2]	Acreage Offered Day of Sale[2]	Parcels Receiving Bids[3]	Acreage Receiving Bids[3]
FY 2015		$143,233,087	1,339	4,077,133	1,286	4,017,062	690	624,976
Wyoming	8/4/2015	$2,006,230	72	70,036	71	69,710	56	50,009
Eastern States	7/28/2015	$198,986	39	16,917	39	16,830	39	16,830
New Mexico	7/22/2015	$70,446,957	72	25,291	69	24,783	69	24,783
Montana/Dakotas	7/14/2015	$39,348	8	1,644	7	1,595	6	1,075
Nevada	6/9/2015	$0	124	256,875	124	256,875	0	0
Idaho	5/28/2015	$3,878,683	5	6,475	5	6,475	5	6,475
Utah	5/19/2015	$277,977	14	15,265	14	15,265	11	13,344
Colorado	5/14/2015	$32,140,365	86	36,195	86	36,195	73	32,962
Montana/Dakotas	5/6/2015	$44,325	3	160	3	160	3	160
Wyoming	5/5/2015	$688,365	35	34,138	31	30,382	31	30,382
Eastern States	3/19/2015	$426,127	11	5,564	11	5,564	11	5,564
Nevada	3/10/2015	$55,383	24	25,882	24	25,882	13	15,244
Utah	2/17/2015	$364,166	53	55,097	17	12,834	17	12,834
Colorado	2/12/2015	$380,892	39	28,079	39	28,079	21	15,281
Wyoming	2/3/2015	$8,551,492	153	157,115	153	157,115	124	121,110
Montana/Dakotas	1/27/2015	$4,256,301	7	1,742	7	1,742	7	1,742
Nevada	12/9/2014	$1,814	100	194,361	97	189,177	1	473
Alaska	11/19/2014	$658,978	270	2,918,189	270	2,918,189	7	66,650
Utah	11/18/2014	$4,983,820	69	72,236	65	64,741	64	64,701
Colorado	11/13/2014	$94,833	24	6,737	24	6,737	19	5,103
Wyoming	11/4/2014	$8,950,306	90	114,385	89	114,142	88	114,102
New Mexico	10/22/2014	$4,102,026	13	19,762	13	19,762	13	19,762
Montana/Dakotas	10/21/2014	$685,713	28	14,988	28	14,828	12	6,390

*Total receipts: The total amount of money generated from the Competitive Oil and Gas Lease Sale. This includes rents, bonuses, and administrative fees.

[1] Parcels and acreage posted: The number of parcels and acreage advertised for sale in the original Notice of Competitive Oil and Gas Lease Sale.

[2] Parcels and acreage offered day of sale: The number of parcels and acreage that were offered for sale at the oral auction.

[3] Parcels and acreage receiving bids: The number of parcels and acreage that received bids and sold at the oral auction.

Note: Parcels offered that did not receive a bid at the oral auction are available for filing of noncompetitive offers (43 CFR 3110.1(b)) for a 2-year period.

Apache Corporation Discovers Significant New Resource Play in Southern Delaware Basin

Apache Corporation NYSE, Nasdaq: APA has announced that after more than two years of extensive geologic and geophysical work, methodical acreage accumulation, and strategic testing and delineation drilling, the company can confirm the discovery of a significant new resource play, the "Alpine High." Apache's Alpine High acreage lies in the southern portion of the Delaware Basin, primarily in Reeves County, Texas. The company estimates hydrocarbons in place on its acreage position are 75 trillion cubic feet Tcf of rich gas more than 1,300 British Thermal Units and 3 billion barrels of oil in the Barnett and Woodford formations alone. Apache also sees significant oil potential in the shallower Pennsylvanian, Bone Springs and Wolfcamp formations.

Key highlights of the discovery:

- Apache has secured 307,000 contiguous net acres 352,000 gross acres at an attractive average cost of approximately $1,300 per acre.

- Alpine High has 4,000 to 5,000 feet of stacked pay in up to five distinct formations including the Bone Springs, Wolfcamp, Pennsylvanian, Barnett and Woodford.

- 2,000 to more than 3,000 future drilling locations have been identified in the Woodford and Barnett formations alone. These formations are in the wet gas window and are expected to deliver a combination of rich gas and oil. Initial estimates for the Woodford and Barnett zones indicate a pretax, net present value NPV range of $4 million to $20 million per well, at benchmark oil and natural gas prices of $50 per barrel and $3 per thousand cubic feet Mcf, respectively. Expected well costs in development mode for a 4,100 foot lateral are estimated to be approximately $4 million per well in normally pressured settings and $6 million per well in over-pressured settings.

- Apache has drilled 19 wells in the play, with nine currently producing in limited quantities due to infrastructure constraints. This includes six wells in the Woodford, one well in the Barnett and one well each in the shallower Wolfcamp and Bone Springs oil formations.

Alpine High play and its large inventory of repeatable, high-value drilling opportunities. We have thousands of low-risk locations in the Woodford and Barnett formations alone, and we are looking forward to further delineating what

October 2016 • Issue 10

we believe will be a significant number of oil-prone locations in the Pennsylvanian, Wolfcamp and Bone Springs."

"This announcement is the culmination of more than two years of hard work by the Apache team. While other companies have focused on acquisitions during the downturn, we took a contrarian approach and focused on organic growth opportunities. These efforts have resulted in the identification of an immense resource that we believe will deliver significant value for our shareholders for many years," said John J. Christmann IV, Apache's chief executive officer and president. "We are incredibly excited about the Alpine High play and its large inventory of repeatable, high-value drilling opportunities.

We have thousands of low-risk locations in the Woodford and Barnett formations alone, and we are looking forward to further delineating what we believe will be a significant number of oil-prone locations in the Pennsylvanian, Wolfcamp and Bone Springs."

"Our announcement represents a significant addition to our already deep and highly economic Permian Basin position. With the contribution of Alpine High to our global portfolio of world-class international and North American assets, Apache clearly has more profitable-growth opportunities than at any other time in the company's 60-year history," Christmann concluded.

BHP BILLITON Paid US$26.7 billion in Economic Contribution and Payments to Governments Globally

BHP Billiton has released its Economic contribution and payments to governments Report which shows the Company's total economic contribution globally in the 2016 financial year was US$26.7 billion. This includes US$3.7 billion globally in taxes, royalties and other payments to governments.

Releasing the report, BHP Billiton Chief Financial Officer Peter Beaven said the Company's adjusted effective tax rate in the 2016 financial year was 35.8 per cent, demonstrating BHP Billiton pays its fair share of tax. When royalties are included, the rate is more than 58 per cent.

"The Company's adjusted effective tax rate averaged 31.9 per cent over the past decade, and 39.8 per cent when royalties

are included," Mr Beaven said. "Over the last decade, our average effective tax rate was higher than the 30 per cent company rate in Australia and the average OECD rate of 25 per cent."

Mr Beaven went on to say that the Report builds on BHP Billiton's commitment to transparency. "Debates about tax need to be informed by facts. It is crucial that the conversation addresses how tax systems take into account the realities of operating in a global economy as well as national interests. This will enable stable investment environments that encourage growth and development," Mr Beaven said.

The Report details payments made to governments during the 2016 financial year on

a country-by-country and project-by-project basis, as well as the significant contribution to suppliers, voluntary contributions to host communities, wages and employee benefits and dividends. It also includes additional information disclosed on a voluntary basis.

In the last decade, BHP Billiton has paid approximately US$85 billion globally in taxes, royalties and other payments to governments, including US$58 billion A$65 billion in Australia.

1 Exploration Success **2** Infrastructure **3** Investor friendly **4** Competitive regime **5** National vision

Equatorial Guinea Government Welcomes Participation in Oil and Gas Licensing Round

A delegation of the Ministry of Mines and Hydrocarbons of Equatorial Guinea has arrived in Singapore to promote the oil and gas licensing round. During the CWC LNG & Gas Series: 8th Asia Pacific Summit, held September 20-23 at the Grand Hyatt in Singapore, the Ministry of Mines and Hydrocarbons welcomes companies to submit letters of interest. EG Ronda 2016, as it is known, will open opportunities for companies in South-East Asia and Australia to take part in the round. H.E. Gabriel Mbaga Obiang Lima, Minister of Mines and Hydrocarbons, said the low cost environment presents the best opportunity to acquire licenses and explore.

"Now is the best time to explore for oil and gas in Equatorial Guinea, when the cost of drilling a well is cheaper and when you have access to a wealth of advanced geological data," said H.E the Minister. "Equatorial Guinea's legacy of exploration success and strong partnerships with international companies create a perfect environment for upstream investment."

 42 **Equatorial Guinea** Drilling Success Rate %

 20 **Global Drilling** Success Rate %

 48 Total Oil & Gas **Discoveries**

 114 Exploration Wells **Drilled**

The Minister made a keynote presentation at 9:05 am on September 21, 2016. The Ministry delegation is available for meetings with interested parties. The MMH invites bids on all open acreage outside of blocks under direct negotiation – 17 licenses in total. EG Ronda 2016 launched on June 6, 2016 at the Africa Oil & Power conference and will conclude on November 30, 2016.

About Equatorial Guinea Licensing Round

Age of Exploration

Equatorial Guinea's ascent to becoming a major African producer was rapid. The Alba field came online in 1991, followed by the game-changing Zafiro field in 1995. The oil boom was well and truly underway, with production rising to a peak of 358,000 barrels daily in 2005.

Six fields and complexes spread across our offshore area produce oil and gas. The most recent to enter production are the Aseng and Alen gas and condensate fields, brought online in 2011 and 2013, respectively. Production of oil, condensate and natural gas products is 342,441 barrels of oil equivalent per day average.

To bolster the upstream industry and to contribute to the growing industrial base in the country, Equatorial Guinea has implemented gas utilization projects that include LNG, methanol and CNG. Block R is due to begin natural gas production in 2020 and will support a floating LNG plant. In order to utilize discovered gas reserves east of Bioko Island, a petrochemicals hub called REPEGE is being developed.

Sustained exploration success has been a hallmark of Equatorial Guinea's upstream oil and gas business, with 48 total discoveries and a drilling success rate of 42 percent. That's almost double the global average.

Production and processing facilities are well established in many parts of the country and seismic data covers large offshore areas. All data will be made available in our data room to interested bidders. The Ministry of Mines and Hydrocarbons now invites oil and gas explorers to bid on a range of prospective acreages, including some unexplored blocks.

Legal Framework

Equatorial Guinea enacted its first Hydrocarbons Law in 1981 Act No. 7/1981. The Constitution of 1995 Act No. 1/1995 applied to this earlier law. Petroleum legislation was updated in 2006 with the introduction of the New Hydrocarbons Law act no. 8/2006, which governs the sector today. In addition to the New Hydrocarbons Law of 2006, companies are subject to the Petroleum Operations Regulation of 2013 and the New Local Content Regulation of 2014, among other directives.

The 2006 Hydrocarbons Law states in Article 1 that all hydrocarbon reservoirs that exist in the surface and subsoil areas of Equatorial Guinea, including its inland waters, territorial waters, exclusive economic zone and continental shelf, are the exclusive property of the state and therefore public domain goods. It also establishes a model production sharing contract.

Directly applicable to companies operating in the petroleum sector are the following laws and regulations:

Tax Law (Act no. 4/2004, of Oct. 28, 2004)

Petroleum Operations Regulation Ministerial Order no. 4/2013

New Local Content Regulation Ministerial Order no. 1/2014

Equatorial Guinea's hydrocarbons legislation states that contracts may be awarded by means of competitive international public tender or direct negotiation. Exploration periods are set at two initial sub-periods of four or five years, plus a maximum of two one-year extensions. The state is entitled to a carried interest participation of not less than 20 percent. Production sharing contracts are the standard petroleum agreement in place.

Chevron to Supply Up to 0.65 Million Metric Tons of Liquefied Natural Gas Annually for 10 years

Chevron Corporation NYSE: CVX has announced that its wholly-owned subsidiary, Chevron U.S.A. Inc., has signed a binding LNG Sales and Purchase Agreement SPA with ENN LNG Trading Company Limited ENN for the delivery of liquefied natural gas LNG to China from Chevron's global supply portfolio. Under the terms of the SPA, ENN will receive up to 0.65 million metric tons per annum MTPA of LNG over 10 years, with the first delivery expected to start in 2018 or the first half of 2019.

"Chevron's commitment to gas is clear. We've been in the natural gas business for more than 100 years, and we're positioned to become one of the top LNG suppliers in the world," said Mike Wirth, executive vice president, Chevron Midstream and Development. "This SPA further demonstrates our work to expand our customer base, our strong customer relationships and our commitment to partnerships around the world."

ENN LNG Trading Company Limited is one of the subsidiaries of ENN Energy Holding Ltd., which is one of the largest natural gas distribution companies in China. ENN Energy Holdings Ltd. operates in 150 cities across 17 provinces and autonomous regions, with over 12 million residential and 56 thousand industrial/commercial customers. ENN's Zhoushan LNG receiving terminal is being constructed and expected to be in operation by 2018.

The SPA delivery requirements are expected to be fulfilled by Chevron's growing LNG portfolio, including the company's Australian LNG interests at Gorgon, Wheatstone and the North West Shelf.

Chevron Corporation is one of the world's leading integrated energy companies. Through its subsidiaries that conduct business worldwide, the company is involved in virtually every facet of the energy industry. Chevron explores for, produces and transports crude oil and natural gas; refines, markets and distributes transportation fuels and lubricants; manufactures and sells petrochemical products; and additives; generates power and produces geothermal energy; and develops and deploys technologies that enhance business value in every aspect of the company's operations.

OPEC Secretary General – Future of energy- Oil and Gas to Remain Dominant, Renewables Do Not Even Come Close

HE Mohammad Sanusi Barkindo, OPEC Secretary General at The European House – Ambrosetti in Italy spoke about, "The future of Energy: Towards a Sustainable Development". According to him, while the future of energy is a future laden with challenges and uncertainties, but also opportunities, one thing stakeholders agree on is the fact that the world will need more energy in the decades to come. It is easy to appreciate why.

In the period to 2040, the global economy is estimated to more than double. And over the same timeframe, world population is projected to reach around 9 billion, an increase of over 1.7 billion from today's level.

And that today around 2.7 billion people still rely on

biomass for their basic needs, and 1.3 billion have no access to electricity. It is vital this is addressed. There is huge potential for socio-economic development in terms of expanding access to modern energy services.

OPEC expect global energy demand to increase by almost 50 per cent by 2040. Energy will be required to power more homes, more services, more businesses, more cars, more planes, more ships … etc.

At the same time, however, stakeholders need to recognize the threat posed by climate change to the environment. He stressed that OPEC welcomes last year's COP 21 agreement in Paris. OPEC Member Countries played a role in drafting the agreement, and they will also play a role in helping implement it.

So while the world will need more energy, it also needs to use it more efficiently and continually look to develop, evolve and adopt cleaner energy technologies.

To put it simply, the basic energy challenge can be summed up in two questions.

The first is how can we ensure there is enough supply

October 2016 • Issue 10

to meet expected future demand growth?

And the second is how this growth can be achieved in a sustainable way, balancing the needs of people in relation to their social welfare, the economy and the environment?

Energy Mix Breakdown

He continued. What is clear is that all forms of energy are required. A diverse mix of sources is the best way forward. However, it is vital to appreciate just what each energy source can provide in the decades ahead.

There is no doubt that renewables, such as solar and wind, will continue to significantly expand their role. OPEC Member Countries recognize and support the development of renewables. Many of OPEC countries have great sources of solar and wind, and significant investments are being made in these fields.

Biomass, nuclear and hydropower are also expected to maintain their share in the global energy mix in the years ahead. Overall, these *renewable energies and nuclear are expected to increase their share in the energy mix from 18 per cent in 2015 to 22 per cent by 2040.*

All of the three main primary sources of energy – oil, gas and coal – will still supply more than three-quarters of the energy mix by 2040. Oil will be at just over 25 per cent, with coal slightly less, and gas slightly more.

From the perspective of oil and gas, it underscores the fact that they will remain central to supplying the growing global population with the critical energy it needs in the decades ahead.

The OPEC Secretary General do not see any outlook predicting that renewables will come close to overtaking oil and gas in the decades ahead.

Is the recent oil price environment is putting this future outlook at risk?

There is no doubt that oil will remain a fuel of choice for the foreseeable future. OPEC sees oil demand increasing by around 17 million barrels a day between now and 2040 to reach close to 110 million barrels a day.

To meet this expansion will require huge investments. OPEC need to consider that new barrels are needed not only to increase production, but to accommodate for decline rates from existing fields. It is estimated that oil-related investment requirements are around $10 trillion in the period to 2040.

It is vital to remember that the short-, medium- and long-term timeframes are all linked. What happens today can have a major bearing on the future. The Industry need to ask itself whether the recent oil price environment is putting this future outlook at risk.

Over the past two years or so the industry has gone through some major readjustments and this had led to a significant drop off in investments. For example, global exploration and production spending fell by around 26 per cent in 2015, and a further 22 per cent drop is anticipated in 2016. Combined this amounts to around $300 billion.

Moreover, according to industry sources, in 2015 explorers discovered only about a tenth as much oil as they have annually on average since 1960. Just 2.7 billion barrels of new supply was discovered in 2015, the smallest amount since 1947.

This is a major concern for an industry that needs regular and predictable investments and output to provide the necessary supply in the medium- and longer terms. *To reverse the declines, oil prices have to go up from recent levels.*

The rebalancing process for the oil market is underway- The industry needs to address the issue of the stock overhang

OPEC remain optimistic that the industry will emerge stronger from these tough times. The industry need to keep in mind that the story of this industry is one of many cycles, both up and down.

But the industry need to remain vigilant, continually monitor the market and the global economy, and do everything it can do to make downward cycles shorter and less extreme. And of course, continue to make the industry ever more efficient in areas such as costs and technologies.

Today, the physical oil market remains in surplus, but it is evident that the rebalancing process is underway.

World economic growth is expected to be 2.9 per cent in 2016 and 3.1 per cent in 2017, although uncertainties such as the impact of the UK's decision to leave the EU and the monetary policies of major central banks will need to be watched closely.

Global oil demand growth is expected to increase by around 1.2 million barrels a day in both 2016 and 2017. And non-OPEC oil supply is anticipated to contract by around 600,000 barrels a day this year, and then increase slightly by 200,000 barrels a day in 2017.

However, there remains a large stock overhang, and

working this off is going to take some time.

Since the end of 2013, OECD commercial stocks have seen their five-year average move from a negative level of 85 million barrels to a surplus of around 340 million barrels today. For the same period there has also been a rise in non-OECD inventories, plus an expansion in some non-OECD strategic petroleum reserves.

These stock increases have been mainly driven by increasing non-OPEC liquids production, which grew by 3.8 million barrels a day in 2014 and 2015. OPEC liquids production grew by only 1.2 million barrels a day over the same period.

The OECD commercial stocks surplus against the five year-average has stabilized this year, but it is important that this starts to reduce. As seen in previous cycles, once this overhang starts falling on a regular basis then prices start to rise.

It is essential both OPEC and non-OPEC producers, as well as consumers, look to address the issue of the **stock overhang. This is now central to the return of a balanced market.**

Concerning the International Energy Forum IEF Ministerial Meeting in Algiers, with all OPEC Member Countries and many non-OPEC producers in attendance. He said, "It is vital for all producers to sit around the table and discuss any possible action that may be required to stabilize the market. And this kind of cooperation needs to be done not only in times of instability, but also when the market is stable and balanced. Dialogue is vital at all times. He was quick to add that the meeting outcome will not necessarily mean that participants will find agreement on everything. But it is important for all stakeholders to find common ground, and look for shared solutions, where and when appropriate.

Over the years OPEC has pushed many forms of energy cooperation, including dialogues with the EU, Russia China and India, symposia and workshops with the IEF and the IEA, various initiatives with the G20, and meetings with other industry stakeholders.

P O G S March 2017

Organized by:

RGT MEDIA COMMUNICATIONS CORP.

The Intl Pipeline Oil and GAS Safety Conference and Exhibition

March 14-16, 2017 Houston Texas USA

Pipeline Integrity | **Emission Reduction** | **Well Control** | **Oil and Gas Transportation** | **Chemical Extraction**

Connecting Supplier with Procurement Teams

Exhibition

200+

Exhibitors Expected

Attendance

2000+

Attendees Expected

Goal

Improve safety in the entire value chain of the oil and gas industry not limited to the well heads but distribution chains, transportation and supply chain.

Exhibit@ P O G S Safety Tech

P O G S Safety Tech provides international and local energy companies who operate across the up, mid and downstream sectors of the oil &gas supply chain with a B2B platform to meet and influence highly-focused International decision-makers and buyers.

Who is Attending?

Take Advantage of Early Registration- Register Now @

http://www.oilandgassafetyconference.com registration/online-registration/

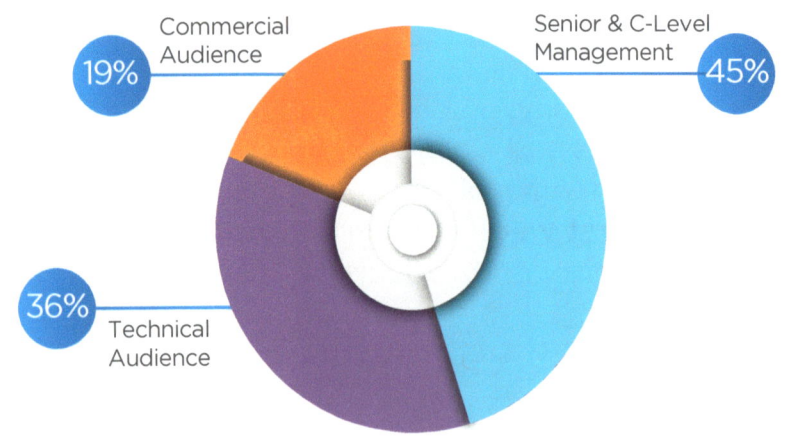

- 19% Commercial Audience
- 45% Senior & C-Level Management
- 36% Technical Audience

Who is Exhibiting?

SHOWFLOOR IS Selling Very Fast RESERVED Today

http://www.oilandgassafetyconference.com/ booth-registeration/

Official Media Partner

For further details visit website @
http://oilandgassafetyconference.com
or call +1-832-664-0618

The International Pipeline, Oil and Gas Safety Conference

POGS March 14-16, 2017   www.oilandgassafetyconference.com

POGS

Intl Pipeline, Oil and Gas Safety Conference & Exhibition

Goals

This conference seeks to address process safety issues in the upstream, midstream and downstream subsectors of the industry; with special focus on well control safety, process safety, pipeline safety, and new regulatory impact.

To help improve operational excellence in the various communities where the industry operates- emerging technologies, leak detection and prevention technologies, emission reduction technologies, compliance audit, best practices to reduce risks and hazards, and improve the overall operational safety is the focal point of this conference.

To help meet these goals - are the speakers and participating companies

Brady Austin
QHSE Service Line Owner Lloyd's Register

Mothusi Pahl
Vice President- Alphabet Energy Inc.

Vincent Higgins
Chairman and CEO Optech4D Inc

Hunter Hawa
Global EHS Director for PSRG

Robert Miller
Regulatory Compliance Specialist, Veriforce

W. Duncan Welder IV
RISC's Director of Client Services

Shoshi Kaganovsky
CEO and founder of SensoLeak

Alexis Vitone
President, AvA Excellence in Business Strategies & HSE, LLC

Tom Meek
Director of Compliance, Veriforce

Keith J. Coyle
Shareholder, Babst Calland

Mark A. Hernandez
President of Multiply Leadership

Rixio Medina
Director of Business Development for the Board of Certified Safety Professionals

Early Registration Fee - $350

Register Today for this all important industrial conference

Fill out this form email form to: *registration@oilandgassafetyconference.com*

Or mail form with check to the address below.

Mail and make check payable to: *RGT Media Communications Corp.   10777 Westheimer Street, #1100 Houston Texas 77042*

Payment Method -Card type- Amex, Visa, Master, Discovery (circle one)

Card No: _____   Expiration Date: _____   Name on card: _____   By Check Check No: _____

First Name: _____   Last Name: _____

Your Preferred Mailing Address - (Circle One) Business/ Residence

Job Title: _____   Company Name : _____   Street : _____

(No PO Boxes Please) City : _____   State: _____   Country: _____   Zip/Postal Code: ___

Day Phone: _____   Fax: _____   E-mail: _____

cut here ✂

Program Agenda Break Down

Pipeline Safety- Leak Detection and Prevention Tech

Shoshi Kaganovsky - CEO and founder of SensoLeak

Emerging Technologies - Leveraging Virtual and Augmented Reality Technologies for Midstream & pipeline industries

Vincent Higgins - Chairman and CEO Optech4D Inc

Best Practices- Avoiding risks and hazards/ Competency-Based Training Program

Alexis Vitone- President - AvA Excellence in Business Strategies & HSE, LLC

Brady Austin - QHSE Service Line Owner- Lloyd's Register

W. Duncan Welder IV - RISC's Director of Client Services

Motivational Speaker

Mark A. Hernandez - President Multiply Leardership

Process Safety

Hunter Hawa - Global EHS Director for PSRG

PHMSA Regulations

Keith J. Coyle - Shareholder- Attorney at Law - Babst Calland

Emission Reduction Technology- Converting Flares to Power Gen

Mothusi Pahl - Vice President-Alphabet Energy Inc.

Compliance Audit- Federal/State codes and OQ NPRM

Tom Meek - Director of Compliance, Veriforce

Robert Miller - Regulatory Compliance Specialist, Veriforce

Rixio Medina - Director of Business Development for the Board of Certified Safety Professionals

---

Supporting Organization

Pennsylvania Independent Oil and Gas Association
PIOGA

Official Media Partner

USA Oil and Gas Monitor

Member Organization

Independent Petroleum Association of America
IPAA

POGS
Intl Pipeline, Oil and Gas
Safety Conference &
Exhibition

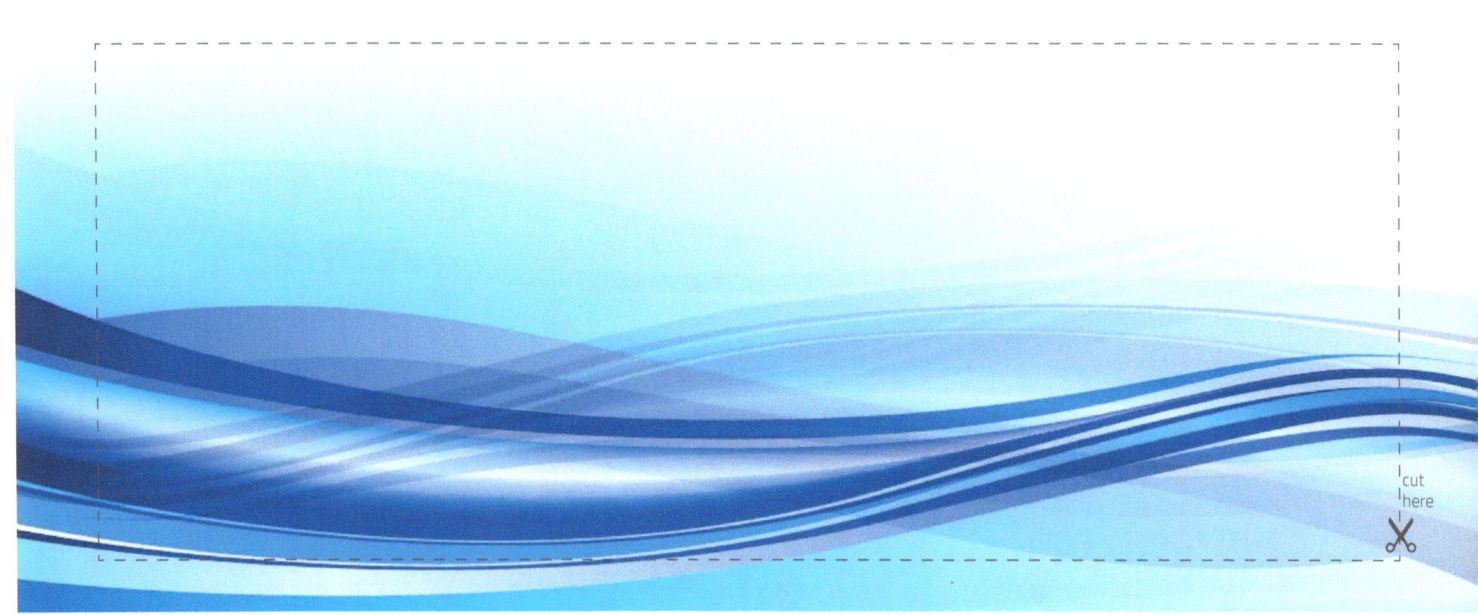

cut
here

October 2016 • Issue 10

USA Oil and Gas Monitor
A RGT Media Communications Corp.

SUBSCRIPTION FORM

First Name _____ Middle _____ Last _____

Current Job Title _____ Job Title Code _____

Company Name _____

Preferred Mailing Address - (Circle One)

  Business   Residence

Street _____ (No PO Boxes Please)

City _____ State _____ Zip _____

Country _____

Day Phone _____ If outside U.S., include country code. (ex: 000-000-000-0000)

Fax _____ Email _____

Form Instructions:

Email completed form to subscribe@usaoilandgasmonitor.com or mail form with check to the address below.

RGT Media Communications Corp.
10777 Westheimer Road #1100
Houston Texas 77042

1 Year Digital Subscription

For non-Texas subscribers - $119.88

Subscribers living in Texas – pays $119.88 plus 8.25% state tax $9.89 = $129.77

1 Year Print Subscription

For non-Texas subscribers - $144

Please add shipping cost and multiply by 12 (for example $1.67 x12) = 20.04

Subscribers living in Texas – pays $144 plus 8.25% state tax $11.88= $155.88

Please add shipping cost and multiply by 12 (for example $1.67 x12) = 20.04

Shipping Cost (calculated by weight)

Circle choice from the following option and add to the subscription cost

First Class 1- 5 business/days = $1.67

Fedex Shipping 1-3 business/days= $6.40

USPS Priority 1-3 business/days= $3.56

International First Class 1-7 business/days= $12.44

You can also pay for subscription online by visiting our website:
www.usaoilandgasmonitor.com/subscribe
Wire transfer, call Jewel Spring, 832-486-0095 for any questions.

Payment Method

Card Type (circle one)

Amex   Visa   Master   Discovery

Card No.

_____

Expiration Date

_____

CSV No.

_____

Name on Card

_____

By Check

Check No.

_____

USA Oil and Gas Monitor
For Daily News Report and Analysis • www.usaoilandgasmonitor.com

October 2016 • Issue 10

U.S Natural Gas Export by Pipeline, LNG Vessel, Truck and CNG- Top Countries and Volumes, Half Year Analysis

U.S. Natural Gas Exports by Country - Six Month Analysis
(Volumes in Million Cubic Feet)

		16-Jan	16-Feb	16-Mar	16-Apr	16-May	16-Jun
Total		168,530	162,762	194,921	176,096	177,343	173,002
	Pipeline	168,479	159,431	184,822	166,031	167,469	156,557
	Canada	69,629	62,192	81,403	63,422	62,768	50,715
	Mexico	98,850	97,240	103,419	102,610	104,701	105,842
	LNG	26	3,309	10,078	10,036	9,874	16,445
	Exports	26	2,019	9,532	10,036	9,874	16,445
	By Vessel	0	1,995	9,507	10,013	9,841	16,423
	Argentina	0	0	0	6,310	0	8,161
	Barbados	0	2	2	3	1	2
	Brazil	0	1,993	3,270	0	0	0
	Chile	0	0	0	0	6,230	4,643
	China	0	0	0	0	0	0
	India	0	0	2,844	0	0	3,617
	Japan	0	0	0	0	0	0
	Kuwait	0	0	0	0	3,610	0
	Portugal	0	0	0	3,700	0	0
	Taiwan	0	0	0	0	0	0
	United Arab Emirates	0	0	3,391	0	0	0
	By Truck	27	24	24	23	33	22
	Canada	2	0	0	0	0	0
	Mexico	25	24	24	23	33	22
	CNG	25	22	21	28	0	0
	Canada	25	22	21	28	0	0

Source EIA- U S. Energy Information Administration

Pipeline Export To Canada and Mexico Jan - June 2016

- 16-Jan 168,530
- 16-Feb 162,762
- 16-Mar 194,921
- 16-Apr 176,096
- 16-May 177,343
- 16-Jun 173,002

Mexico Largest Importer of U. S. Natural Gas by Pipeline

The United States Natural Gas Export by pipeline shows that the month of March has the highest export of 194,921, followed by 177,343 in May, 176,096 in April, 173,002 in June, 168,530 in January and 162,762 in February. 67 per cent, or 612,662 of the total U.S natural gas export by pipeline goes to Mexico while 33 per cent or 390,129 is exported to Canada.

Argentina Largest Consumer of U. S. LNG Export by Vessel

U.S natural gas export by LNG vessel was exported to the following countries. Argentina, Barbados, Brazil, Chile, China, India, Japan, Kuwait, Portugal, Taiwan and United Arab Emirates. Argentina received the highest volume of U. S. LNG export, a total of 14,471mcf in six month, which is 6,310 and 8,161 in April and June respectively. Followed by Chile with a total volume of 10,873, which is 6,230 and 4,643 in May and June respectively. India received a total of 6,461, which is 2,844 and 3,617 in March and June respectively. Brazil received a total of 5,263, which is 1,993 and 3,270 in February and March respectively. Portugal received 3,700 in April only. Kuwait 3,610 in May only, and United Arab Emirates, 3,391 in March only. Taiwan and Japan did not receive any export during this time.

LNG Export Vessel By Country Jan- June 2016

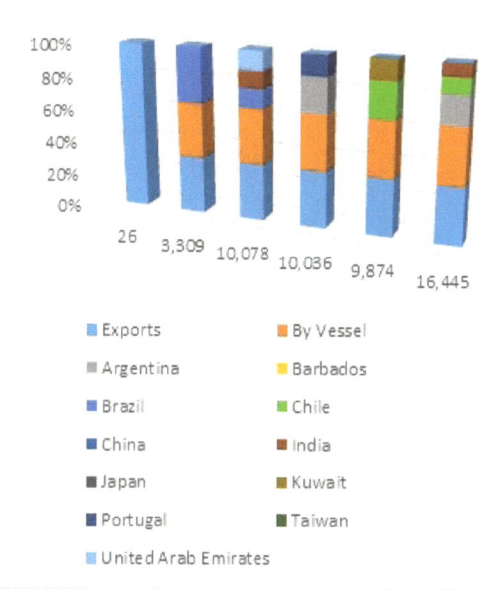

26   3,309   10,078   10,036   9,874   16,445

- Exports
- By Vessel
- Argentina
- Barbados
- Brazil
- Chile
- China
- India
- Japan
- Kuwait
- Portugal
- Taiwan
- United Arab Emirates

October 2016 • Issue 10

US Natural Gas Export By Truck To Canada and Mexico Jan-June 2016

Mexico No 1 Destination for U. S. Natural Gas Export by Truck

U.S natural gas export by truck in the period in review shows that only 2 trucks move natural gas to Canada in the January; no other truck moved natural gas for the remainder period. Whereas, Mexico received a total of 151 natural gas export by truck during this period.

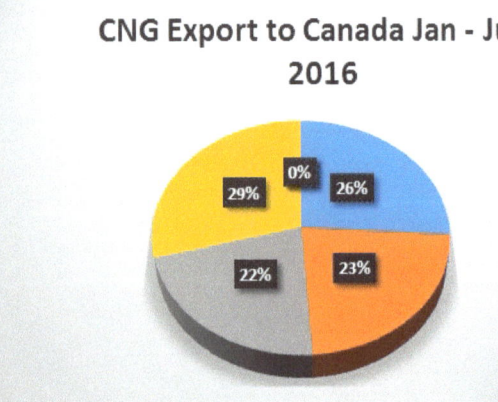

CNG Export to Canada Jan - June 2016

Canada Top Destination for U. S. Natural Gas Export by CNG

CNG, Compressed Natural Gas export to Canada totaled 196 during this period.

Pipeline Shutdown Disrupts Gasoline Supply in the Southeast

A partial shutdown of the Colonial Pipeline system, a major source transportation fuels supply to the Southeast, has disrupted gasoline supplies, leading to higher prices and product shortages in parts of the region.

Colonial Pipeline shut down its "Line 1" pipeline in response to a leak near the town of Pelham in Shelby County, Alabama. Repair and restoration activities are currently underway, including the construction of a 500-foot, above-ground bypass around the affected section of pipeline. The bypass is expected to allow the pipeline to resume operations and flow rates on "Line 1" immediately.

Colonial Pipeline is a significant source of transportation fuels supply for several southeastern states particularly Georgia, South Carolina, North Carolina, and Virginia and Tennessee. The U.S. Southeast accounts for approximately 12 per cent of total U.S. motor gasoline consumption and 34 per cent of Petroleum Administration for Defense District PADD 1 consumption. Because there are no refineries between Alabama and Pennsylvania that produce substantial quantities of transportation fuels, the U.S. Southeast is supplied primarily via pipeline flows from refineries along the Gulf Coast supplemented by marine shipments from the Gulf Coast and imports.

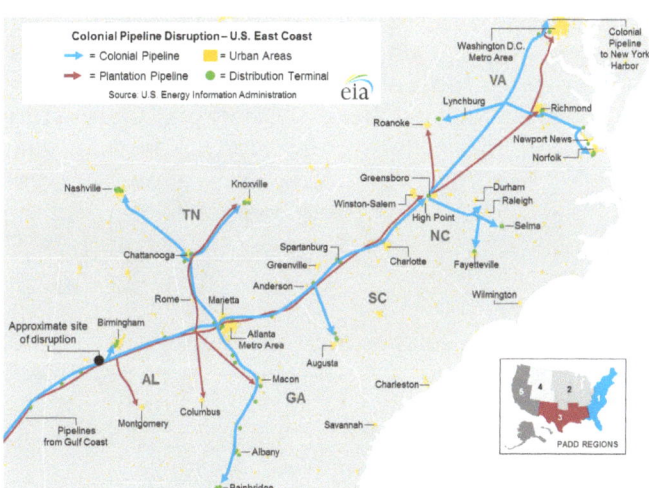

Colonial Pipeline is a 2.5 million barrel per day b/d system of approximately 5,500 miles of pipeline. The pipeline connects 29 refineries and 267 distribution terminals, carrying refined petroleum products such as gasoline, diesel, heating oil, and jet fuel from as far west as Houston, Texas to as far north as New York Harbor. Various branches of Colonial Pipeline supply markets in central and eastern Tennessee, southern Georgia, and eastern and western portions of Virginia. "Line 1" carries approximately 1.4 million b/d of gasoline from the Gulf Coast to a major junction and storage hub in Greensboro, North Carolina. From Greensboro,

October 2016 • Issue 10

two pipelines carry a mix of fuels further north to Maryland and Linden, New Jersey, near New York Harbor. Colonial Pipeline consistently runs at full capacity, as pipeline movements are the lowest cost delivery mechanism into the area.

As Colonial Pipeline works to restore service on "Line 1," gasoline shipments were temporarily dispatched on its "Line 2" pipeline, which normally carries only diesel fuel, heating oil, and jet fuel, in order to deliver incremental supplies to Greensboro, North Carolina. However, the gasoline supplies were less than the volumes that would normally be transported on "Line 1," and they displaced distillate supplies that would normally be shipped on "Line 2." Gasoline, diesel, and other fuels also continue to be delivered via Plantation Pipeline, the other major refined products pipeline transporting supplies from the Gulf Coast to as far north as Virginia. However, it is much smaller in capacity, approximately 700,000 b/d, and, like the Colonial system, normally runs at full capacity.

Affected markets will seek alternative supply arrangements, which will vary by market and location. Inland markets in the Southeast that depend heavily on Colonial Pipeline do not have easy access to alternative supply sources other than long-distance trucking from distant supply points. Markets along the East Coast with access to deep-water ports, such as Savanah, Georgia; Charleston, South Carolina; Wilmington, North Carolina; and Norfolk, Virginia, can receive limited imports from the global market and marine shipments via coastwise compliant shipping originating in the U.S. Gulf Coast.

In an effort to make additional supplies available, federal and state governments have issued regulatory waivers and notices. The U.S. Environmental Protection Agency issued waivers that allow

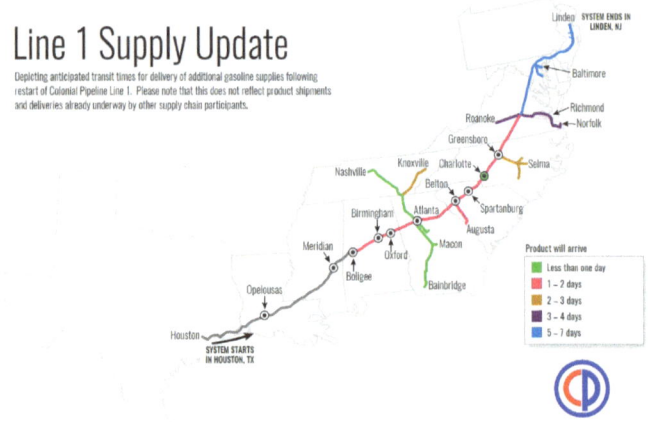

Line 1 Supply Update

Depicting anticipated transit times for delivery of additional gasoline supplies following restart of Colonial Pipeline Line 1. Please note that this does not reflect product shipments and deliveries already underway by other supply chain participants.

conventional gasoline to be sold in metropolitan areas that normally require reformulated gasoline, as well as waivers for Reid vapor pressure specifications. Additionally, as of September 16, six states have issued waivers on hours-of-service restrictions for truck drivers delivering gasoline, allowing for longer-distance transportation.

Until gasoline supplies again arrive via Colonial Pipeline, affected distribution terminals will rely on their current stocks and supplies obtained from alternative sources. Because shipments of gasoline in pipelines move slowly, at approximately five miles per hour, some markets may still be experiencing supply shortfalls several days after service is restored on Colonial Pipeline, however, alternative supply arrangements would continue during that time.

Any limitation in the availability of gasoline at local distribution terminals will be reflected in their posted "rack" prices, which, combined with the higher costs of alternative supply options, will ultimately influence the retail price of gasoline. On September 19, the average retail price of regular gasoline increased eight cents from the previous week to $2.17 per gallon in PADD 1C, a region that includes several states along the southern Atlantic coast.

For the week ending September 16, total U.S. motor gasoline inventories fell by just over 3 million barrels; this masks significant regional variations, however. Because the Colonial Pipeline is a major outlet for Gulf Coast refinery gasoline production, the current disruption caused supplies to back up or be stranded along the Gulf Coast to the extent that coastwise maritime shipments or export markets are unable to absorb the extra volumes. Therefore, while gasoline stocks at affected distribution terminals in the

Petroleum Administration for Defense Districts

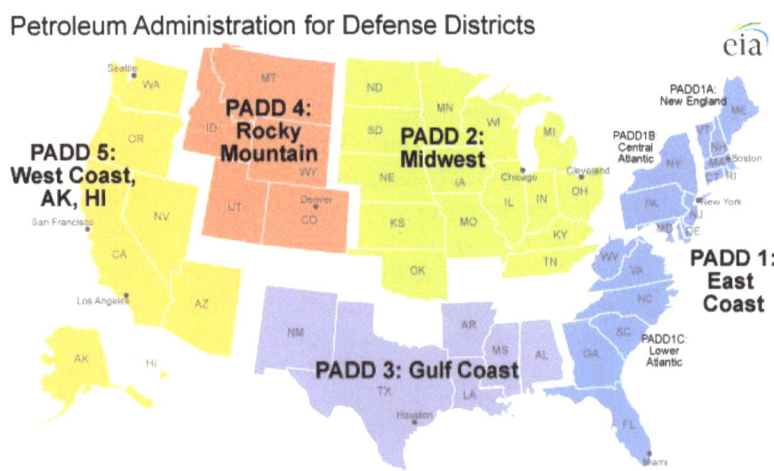

Southeast were drawn down during the disruption, gasoline stocks in the Gulf Coast region rose.

As expected, the Southeast showed the largest decline, with gasoline inventories down roughly 6 million barrels for the week from a base of roughly 28 million barrels. The Mid-Atlantic region PADD 1B, which includes the New York Harbor area, showed a decline of just over 2 million barrels about 6 per cent. Conversely, the Gulf Coast region showed an increase in gasoline inventories of nearly 5 million barrels.

The decreases in Southeast gasoline inventories were at both terminals and pipelines. Of the roughly 150 terminals sampled on a weekly basis in the Southeast, 120 showed declines in gasoline inventories for the week ending September 16. There

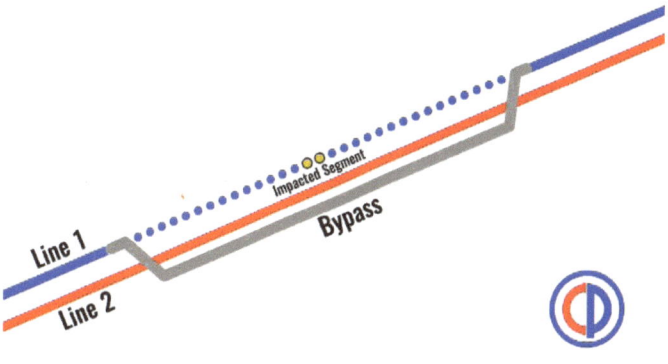

were no significant changes in refinery operations on either the East Coast or Gulf Coast, and there was no sizable change to import volumes to the East Coast.

First Shipment of Ethane from U.S. Gulf Coast arrives in Europe

The first U.S. ethane export terminal, located in Marcus Hook, Pennsylvania, about 20 miles southwest of Philadelphia, has an export capacity of 35,000 barrels per day b/d and began shipping ethane cargos in March 2016. The second U.S. ethane export terminal, opened by Enterprise Products Partners in Morgan's Point, Texas, recently sent its first shipment to Norway. This 200,000 b/d-capacity facility, located on the Houston Ship Channel, is the first ethane terminal in the Gulf Coast region.

Ineos Olefins and Polymers Europe, with ethylene cracker operations in Scotland and Norway, and its partner Evergas, a company specializing in seaborne petrochemical and liquid gas transportation, took delivery of the first ship in a planned eight-vessel fleet of Large Gas Carriers LGC. These vessels will primarily transport ethane produced in the Marcellus and Utica shale plays to Europe from the Mariner East project/Marcus Hook Industrial Center in Pennsylvania, under a 15-year contract between Ineos-Europe and Evergas.

The Marcus Hook Industrial Complex, located along the Delaware River south of Philadelphia, Pennsylvania, was formerly a Sunoco refinery and is now being used as a terminal and dock facility. It is operated by Sunoco Logistics Partners, with additional hydrocarbon gas liquids HGL related manufacturing, including a planned propane dehydrogenation plant. The Mariner East 1 and Mariner East 2 pipeline projects are designed to

Dragon Class 27,500 m3 liquid gas carrier intended for transatlantic shipments of Marcellus ethane

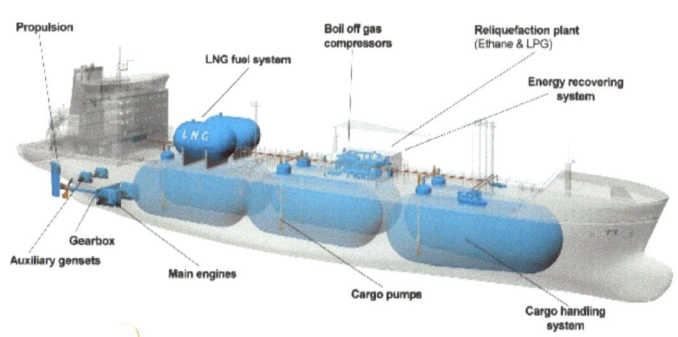

eia   Source: Wärtsilä USA.

deliver HGL from the Marcellus and Utica shale areas in western Pennsylvania, West Virginia, and eastern Ohio to Marcus Hook. Mariner East 1 began operations in fourth-quarter 2014, delivering propane to Marcus Hook, and is scheduled to be fully operational for delivering up to 70,000 b/d of propane and ethane in the second half of 2015. Mariner East 2 is expected to begin operations in fourth-quarter 2016 with an initial capacity of 275,000 b/d for both domestic and international customers.

With the first Dragon class vessel entering operation, and Ineos upgrading its ethane terminal in Rafnes, Norway. These ships measure 591 feet ft long, 87 ft wide, and have a draft of 30 ft. They are the largest ethane carriers in production to date and have a

October 2016 • Issue 10

rated capacity of 971,162 cubic feet, or 175,000 barrels. These ships are designated as the Dragon class, and are identified by Evergas as among the most technologically advanced liquid gas carriers on the seas today. Manufactured by Sinopacific Offshore & Engineering, a shipyard in China, these LGCs use LNG for propulsion and cargo handling, systems supplied by Wärtsilä, a Finnish manufacturer, to optimize performance for ship's systems and cargo management.

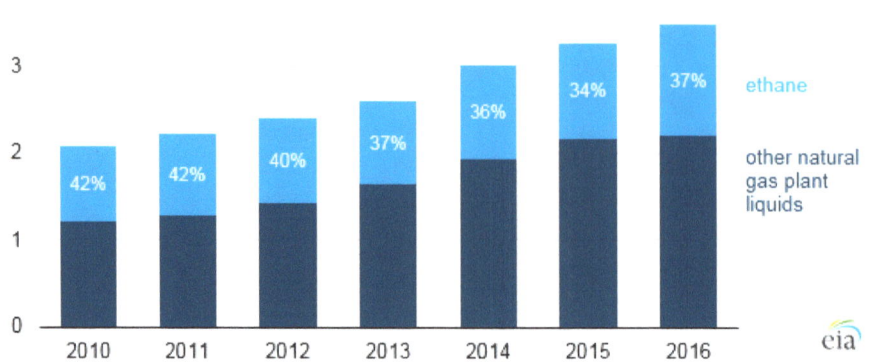

Production of ethane and other natural gas plant liquids (2010-16)
million barrels per day

Increased production of ethane in the United States has led to increased ethane exports, first by pipeline to Canada and more recently by tanker to overseas destinations. Ethane is used domestically and internationally as a key feedstock for plastics production and other industrial uses.

Ethane is typically extracted from unprocessed natural gas, along with other natural gas plant liquids NGPL. Unlike heavier natural gas plant liquids—such as propane, butanes, and natural gasoline—significant amounts of ethane can be left in natural gas transported on pipelines to natural gas customers, a practice known as ethane rejection. The relative tendency to either reject or recover ethane i.e., leave it in the natural gas stream or separate it and market it, depends on ethane prices and demand and the ability of facilities to remove ethane from raw natural gas.

Because ethane has a higher heat content than methane—the primary component of natural gas—higher heat content of a natural gas stream often indicates that ethane is being rejected, or left in the natural gas sold to natural gas users. EIA has collected monthly data on natural gas heat content by state since 2013. The heat content of natural gas in states that receive shale gas produced from the Marcellus and Utica formations, such as Ohio, Maryland, Delaware, and Pennsylvania, has been consistently reported at or above national average levels. Ohio, in particular, receives a higher portion of its natural gas from the Marcellus and Utica formations. However, since early 2016, the natural gas heat content in these states has trended downward, indicating that producers have increasingly been extracting ethane. The lower heat content has coincided with the start of ethane exports out of Marcus Hook, which sources all of its ethane from the Marcellus and Utica formations. From 2010 to 2015, the ethane share of total NGPL production dropped from 42 per cent to 34per cent. Although other natural gas plant liquids have found ready markets close to key shale plays such as the Marcellus and Utica formations, the lack of pipelines and local markets for ethane in these areas has limited ethane recovery.

With more export capability and growth in domestic petrochemical demand, more ethane is expected to be recovered and brought to market. EIA's Short-Term Energy Outlook projects NGPL production to continue growing, from 3.6 million barrels per day b/d in May 2016 to 4.0 million b/d in December 2017. Nearly half of the projected total increase in NGPL production is ethane. Although an expectation of increasing oil prices and an associated increase in NGPL prices contributes to the outlook, a major driver of increased ethane production is growth in ethane demand, both within the United States and internationally.

Major structural and tectonic features in the region of the Utica play

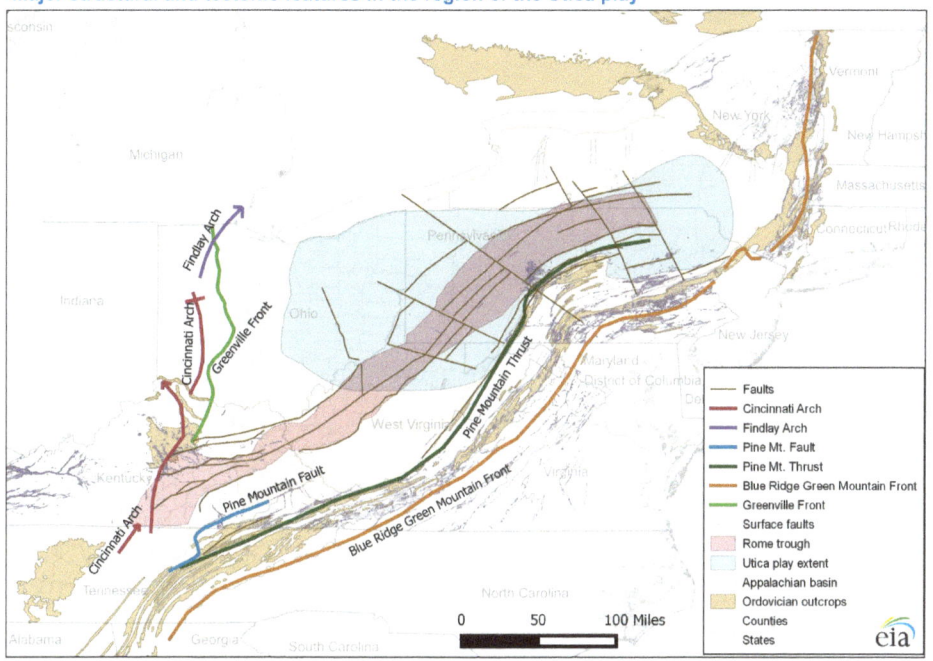

Source: U.S. Energy Information Administration, based on DrillingInfo Inc., IHS Inc., The Appalachian Oil and Natural Gas Research Consortium, and U.S. Geological Survey.

Utica Play Natural Gas-Rich Areas an Increasingly Target For Hydrocarbon Production

Production of oil and natural gas in the Appalachian Basin's Utica play—which includes both the Utica and Point Pleasant formations—has increased significantly since 2012. Monthly natural gas production from Utica wells increased from 0.1 billion cubic feet per day Bcf/d in December 2012 to more than 3.5 Bcf/d in June 2016. Oil production increased from 4,400 barrels per day b/d to nearly 76,000 b/d over the same period.

2012 natural gas Production 0.1bcf

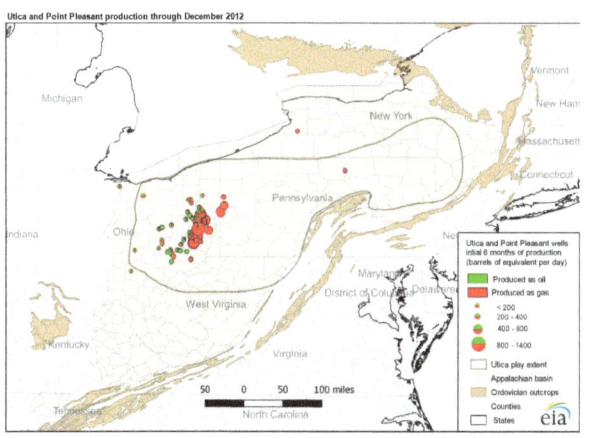

2016 natural gas Production over 3.5bcf

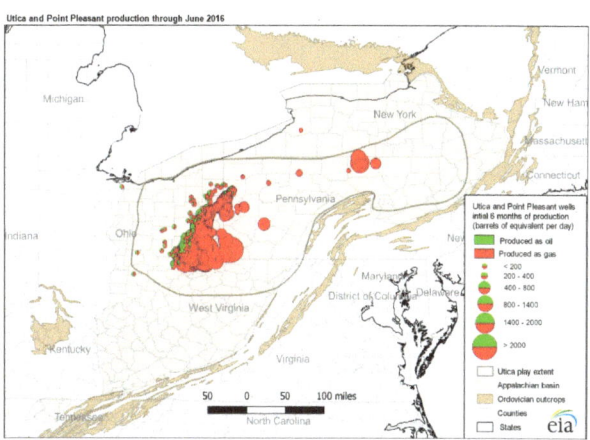

October 2016 • Issue 10

Only 104 wells in the Utica play produced oil or natural gas in 2012, with most wells coming into production in 2013 or later, as shown on the maps above. Although the Utica play produces a mixture of oil and natural gas, recent development in the Utica has focused on natural gas. The rapid growth in Utica/Point Pleasant natural gas production since 2012 is attributable to increases in drilling efficiency, proximity to markets, improvements in business processes, resource targeting in stacked plays, and the lengthening of horizontal laterals. Relatively low oil prices and expansions in natural gas infrastructure make the natural gas-rich portions of the reservoir more desirable for development, and

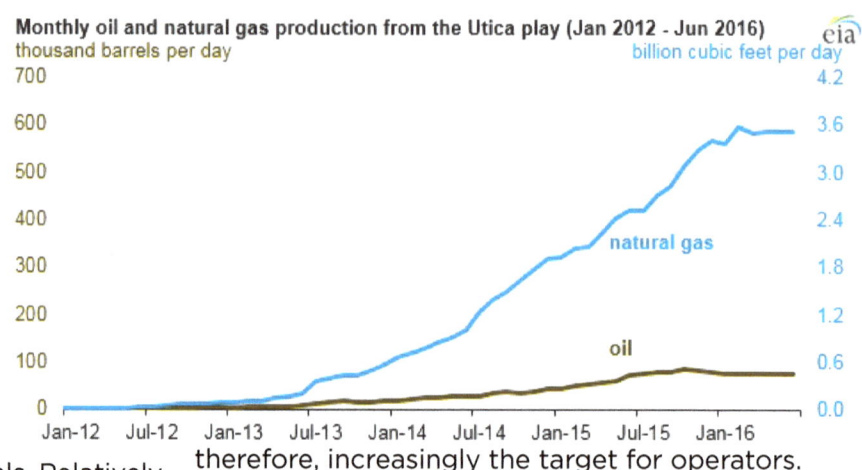

Monthly oil and natural gas production from the Utica play (Jan 2012 - Jun 2016)

therefore, increasingly the target for operators.

Depth to the top of Utica formation in feet and thermal maturity

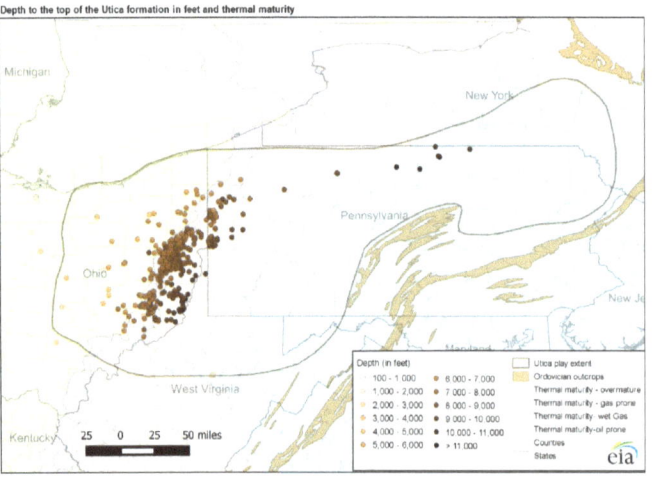

Initial gas-to-oil ratios GOR of Utica and pleasant well and thermal maturity

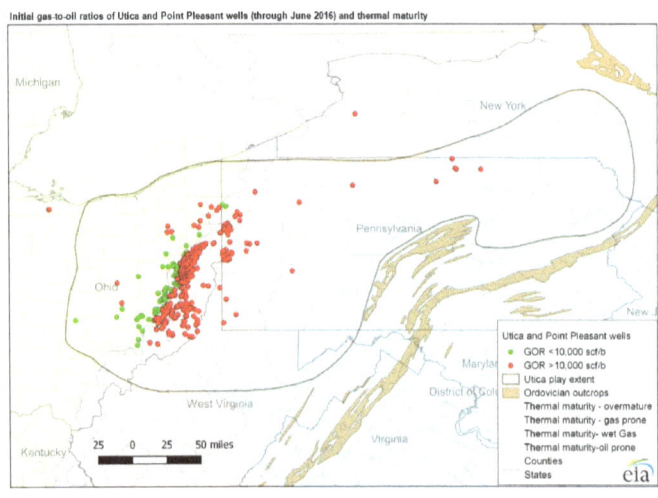

The relative portions of natural gas and oil in a particular formation can be represented by mapping initial gas-to-oil ratios GORs. GORs characterize the ratio of natural gas to oil produced from a well, expressed in standard cubic feet per barrel—scf/b. The distribution of oil and natural gas in a formation is partially controlled by the thermal maturity of a rock, which is an indication of potential hydrocarbon generation.

Crude oil and natural gas are produced by the heating of organic materials i.e., kerogen found in some rocks over long periods of time. When organic-rich rocks, usually shales, are buried, they are exposed to increasing temperatures and pressures. Heating causes the organic matter to change into the waxy material known as kerogen, then into oil, and finally into natural gas as the temperature further increases.

The temperature ranges conducive to converting organic material to oil and natural gas are referred to as the oil window and the gas window, respectively. The oil window typically occurs at temperatures between 60 degrees and 120 degrees Celsius, while the natural gas window occurs between 100 degrees and 200 degrees Celsius. Although this temperature range is found at different depths below the surface throughout the world, a typical depth for the oil window in the Utica play is 4,000 feet to 8,000 feet, and the corresponding gas window is 7,000 feet to 12,000 feet.

In the map above, natural gas-rich wells in the Utica play are mostly located in the eastern portion of the play, and oil-rich wells are typically located in the western portion. The distribution of initial GORs generally corresponds to the depth of the reservoir. Deeper wells up to 13,000 feet in the eastern portion have higher initial GORs greater than 10,000 scf/b and produce mostly natural gas, while the shallower wells to the west have lower initial GORs less than 10,000 scf/b and produce mostly oil.

The U.S. Department of State's Energy Resource Bureau ENR in partnership with the Blum Center for Developing Economies at UC Berkeley hosted the Silicon Valley Tech Challenge: Accelerating Access to Clean Energy Around the World.

Over 1 billion people globally lack access to electricity and another billion lack access to reliable electricity. Providing access to energy can enable progress across the education, health, social, and economic sectors. Innovative and scalable solutions are needed to meet the drastically rising demand for electricity across the developing world, as well as the urgent imperative to significantly reduce global carbon emissions.

The Accelerating Access to Clean Energy Around the World workshop convened key stakeholders from across Silicon Valley — including tech companies, investors, foundations, non-governmental organizations, government, and academia — to develop new and further innovate current technological approaches to tackling this challenge. Barriers to accelerating access were identified at a smaller workshop at the June 2016 Global Entrepreneurship Summit in Palo Alto convened by the U.S. Department of State.

This larger workshop focused on generating ambitious and impactful

Silicon Valley Tech Challenge:
Accelerating Access to Clean Energy around the World

proposals to overcome those barriers, bringing together not just experts in renewable energy but also those on the cutting-edge of intersecting technology trends, such as expanding internet access, mobile payments and platforms, cloud storage, and data analytics. Additionally, ENR brought 15 clean energy entrepreneurs from Asia and Africa to provide on-the-ground perspective.

A number of companies and organizations who participated in the workshop will either be furthering ideas and solutions that were generated or identifying and launching initiatives to address key challenges to off-grid clean energy access, including Microsoft, X formerly GoogleX, Facebook, Orange Silicon Valley, Booz Allen Hamilton, Galvanize, Bloomberg New Energy Finance, DBL Partners, Allotrope Partners, Factor[E] Ventures, IdeaScale, Powerhouse, Singularity University, Afriji, and UC Berkeley's Blum Center for Developing Economies, Sutardja Center for Entrepreneurship and Technology, and Haas School of Business.

This event was part of the State Department's recently-launched Innovation Forum and Silicon Valley presence, with a mission to build bridges between policymakers and innovators to tackle the most pressing global challenges.

October 2016 • Issue 10

U.S. Crude Oil Exports to 16 Countries and Canada

In recent years, crude oil exports to destinations other than Canada were often re-exported volumes of foreign crude oil or cargoes of Alaskan crude oil, which were both exempt from export restrictions. The number and variety of destinations for U.S. crude oil exports has increased since the lifting of restrictions in December 2015. So far in 2016, U.S. crude oil has been exported to 16 different nations, totaling 501,000 b/d.

U.S. crude oil exports have occurred despite relatively small price spreads between international crude oils and domestic crude oils, as well as other factors that should reduce crude oil exports such as falling U.S. crude oil production and added cargo export costs.

Based on the latest available data, U.S. crude oil exports averaged 501,000 barrels per day b/d in the first five months of 2016, 43,000 b/d 9 per cent more than the full-year 2015 daily average. U.S. exports of crude oil had already increased significantly before the lifting of crude oil export restrictions. These exports were mostly to Canada, which was excluded from the previous restrictions. From 2000 to 2013, U.S. exports rarely surpassed 100,000 b/d. By 2015, the United States was exporting 422,000 b/d to Canada and a total of 26,000 b/d to five other countries.

U.S. crude oil exports to countries other than Canada have surpassed exports to Canada in two months in 2016. In March, total crude oil exports to countries other than Canada reached 259,000 b/d, or 10,000 b/d more than crude oil exports to Canada. In May, total U.S. crude oil exports to countries other than Canada reached 354,000 b/d, 46,000 b/d more than crude oil exports to Canada.

Other than Canada, the largest and most consistent U.S. crude oil export destination for the first five months of 2016 has been Curacao, an island nation located in the Caribbean Sea north of Venezuela. U.S. crude oil exports to Curacao averaged 54,000 b/d through May. Petróleos de Venezuela PDVSA, the state-owned oil company of Venezuela, operates the 330,000 b/d Isla refinery on Curacao, as well as crude and petroleum product storage facilities on the island. Trade press reports indicate that U.S. crude oil exports to Curacao are likely being used as diluent, where a light less dense U.S. crude oil is blended with a heavy Venezuelan crude oil, for either processing at the Isla refinery or for re-export to PDVSA customers.

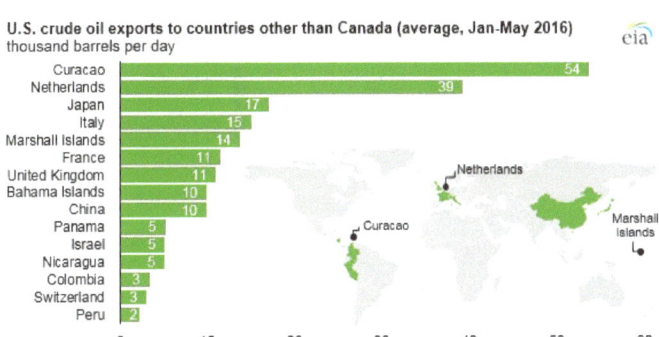

U.S. crude oil exports to countries other than Canada (average, Jan-May 2016)
thousand barrels per day

Source: U.S. Energy Information Administration, Petroleum Supply Monthly

Exports to the Netherlands, the second-largest non-Canadian destination for U.S. crude oil, averaged 39,000 b/d through the first five months of this year. Two of the three cities that collectively are the large refining and petroleum product trading hub of Amsterdam, Rotterdam, and Antwerp, known as the ARA, are located in the Netherlands. Other Western European nations, including Italy, France, and the United Kingdom, also rank high on the list of U.S. crude oil export destinations.

The Marshall Islands, a group of islands in the Pacific Ocean, is the fifth-largest non-Canadian destination for U.S. crude oil exports in 2016, averaging 14,000 b/d through May. With no refineries, the Marshall Islands are unlikely the final destination, but rather may be the location of ship-to-ship transfers for delivery to destinations in Asia, or a point at which a cargo of crude oil would await a buyer in Asia. U.S. Customs and Border Protection documentation requires the final destination of an export, if known. Therefore, cargoes that will undergo ship-to-ship transfer or that do not have a buyer prior to loading will cite the jurisdiction of the transfer, not the cargo's actual final destination.

The costs involved in exporting a cargo of crude oil can vary significantly. Transporting crude to a port, storage, loading, shipping, and other costs typically require large price spreads to make a transaction economic. Recent exports are occurring during a period when the price of Brent crude oil, the benchmark for global seaborne crude has held a narrow premium to West Texas Intermediate WTI, the U.S. benchmark, limiting the positive economic options for exporting U.S. crude. Through early August 2016, WTI averaged about $0.31 per barrel less than Brent, despite a recent widening to $1.08/b for the week ending July 1

Available shipping options can provide opportunities for crude exports despite a narrow price spread. For example, the recent cost of booking a tanker for a spot shipment of crude oil has been the lowest since 2009. Also, if either a buyer or a seller of exported crude oil has a tanker on time charter, meaning the vessel's time has already been paid for a set period, fixing its cost, the vessel may operate independently of tanker rates. Another shipping option is to book a back-haul voyage, the trip a tanker would normally make empty while returning to a port to load its next cargo. Back-haul voyages can be significantly discounted from regular tanker rates. Refineries in the ARA and in the rest of Western Europe actively trade with markets and refineries in the United States, using both clean, refined cargoes and dirty less refined or unrefined cargoes tankers. Trade flows between Europe and the U.S. Gulf Coast, which primarily use dirty tankers for transporting crude and less refined products such as residual fuel oil, provide opportunities for back-haul cargoes of U.S. crude oil.

In addition, sellers of U.S. crude can use several methods to entice buyers despite unfavorable price spreads. A particular cargo or grade of crude oil can be discounted from a benchmark based on quality variations, such as API gravity, sulfur content, or other specifications. With the hope of continued purchases in the future, marketers of U.S. crude for export may offer buyers price discounts on sample or test cargoes, so that refiners may become more familiar with the crude and its compatibility with their refinery and desired product yield. This may explain some of the sporadic, typically small-volume crude oil export patterns to some countries in Asia, Europe, and elsewhere.

Sustained and significant increases in U.S. crude oil exports, however, likely require more than lower shipping costs and sporadic purchases. It would require increased U.S. crude oil production and a significantly wider Brent-WTI price spread, neither of which are projected in EIA's August Short-Term Energy Outlook.